I dedicated this book to my dad, who took me to my first game.

ISBN: 978-0-578-43188-8

Edited by Lisa Gallo Roth

Baseball Dream

Written by Renée Nolte
Illustrated by Al Salgado

This Book Belongs to:

----

*T*ake me out to the ballgame,
take me out to the crowd.
Buy me some peanuts and Cracker Jack,
I don't care if I ever get back.
Let me *root, root, root* for the home team,
if they don't win, it's a shame.
For it's one, two, three strikes you're out
at the **old ball game!**

What do you like about baseball?...'Cause I'm ALWAYS in a Baseball Dream.

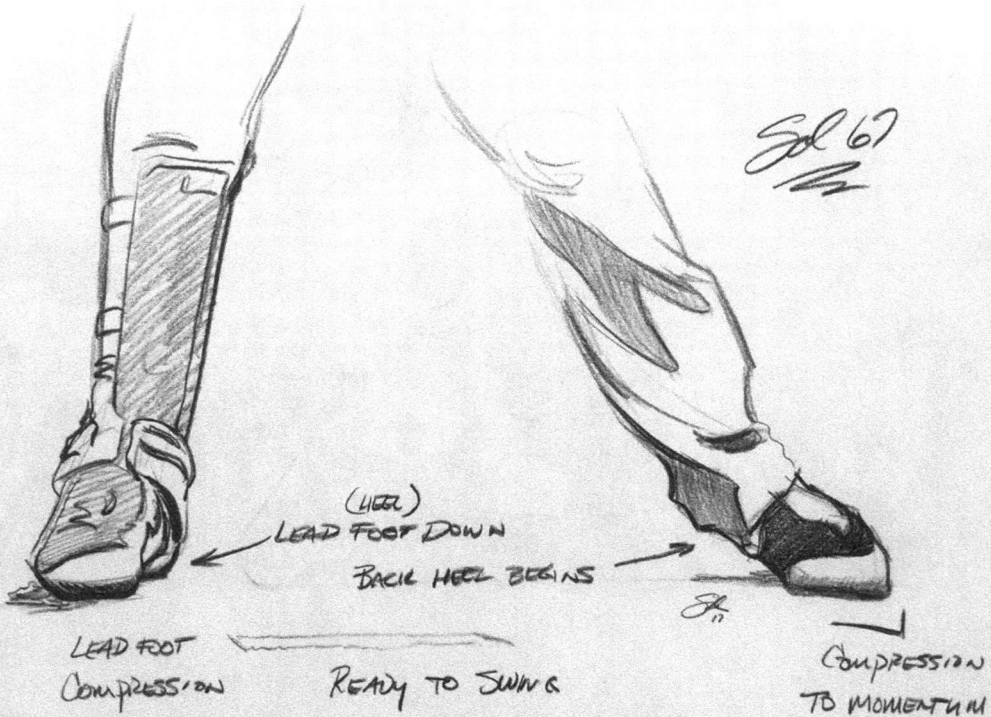

(HEEL)
LEAD FOOT DOWN
BACK HEEL BEGINS

LEAD FOOT
COMPRESSION   READY TO SWING

COMPRESSION
TO MOMENTUM

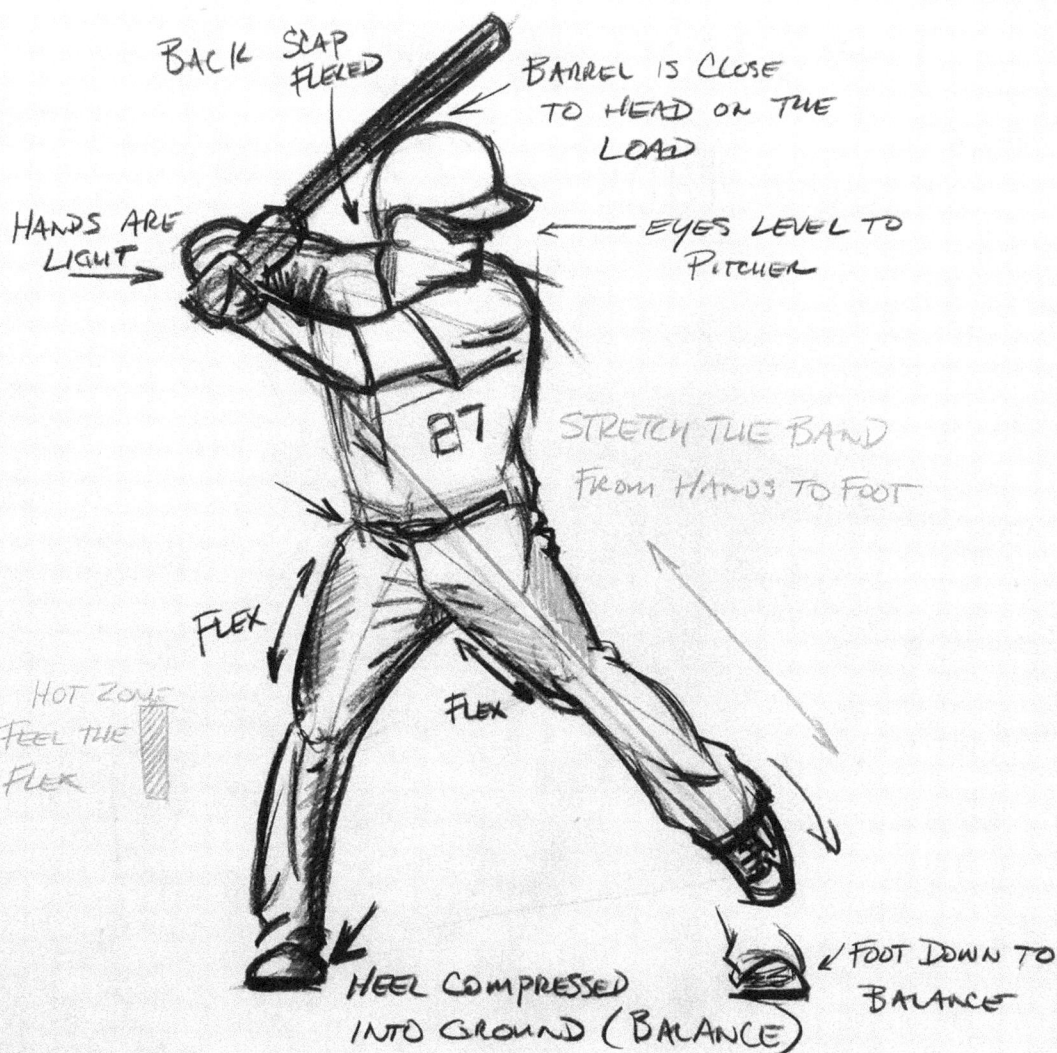

W hat do YOU like about baseball?

Is it the club,
 the history,
  the fans?

Do you like the songs?
Do you hum them all night
long?

Dun dun dun dun

Dun dun dun dun

Dun dun dun dun

Score!!!

Do you like the sport?
Do you *Sport* it
all day long?

Do you like the ballcaps?

Do you like the *logos*?

Do you wear jerseys from your favorite teams?

Is **baseball** part of your clothes?

Do you have a favorite number?

Who's your *Faaaavorite* baseball guy?

Do you remember your first
game with a twinkle in your eye?

*D*o you like baseball history?
Do you like to see history made?

Do you *honor* the legends of those in
the *Baseball Hall of Fame*?

What's your favorite *Baseball* position?

What do you like to see played...

...a *P*itcher who curves,
...a *R*unner who steals

TROUT 27

...an *O*utfielder who
jumps in the game?

Do you like the...

Bases Loaded

when the last player is up to bat?

I guess it depends on your team, because it will be grand for a *Home Run* like that!

What do you see from the coaches, nodding secret codes

All Game?

What about the dug out and the players, blowing bubbles, spitting seeds out, watching AND waiting to play?

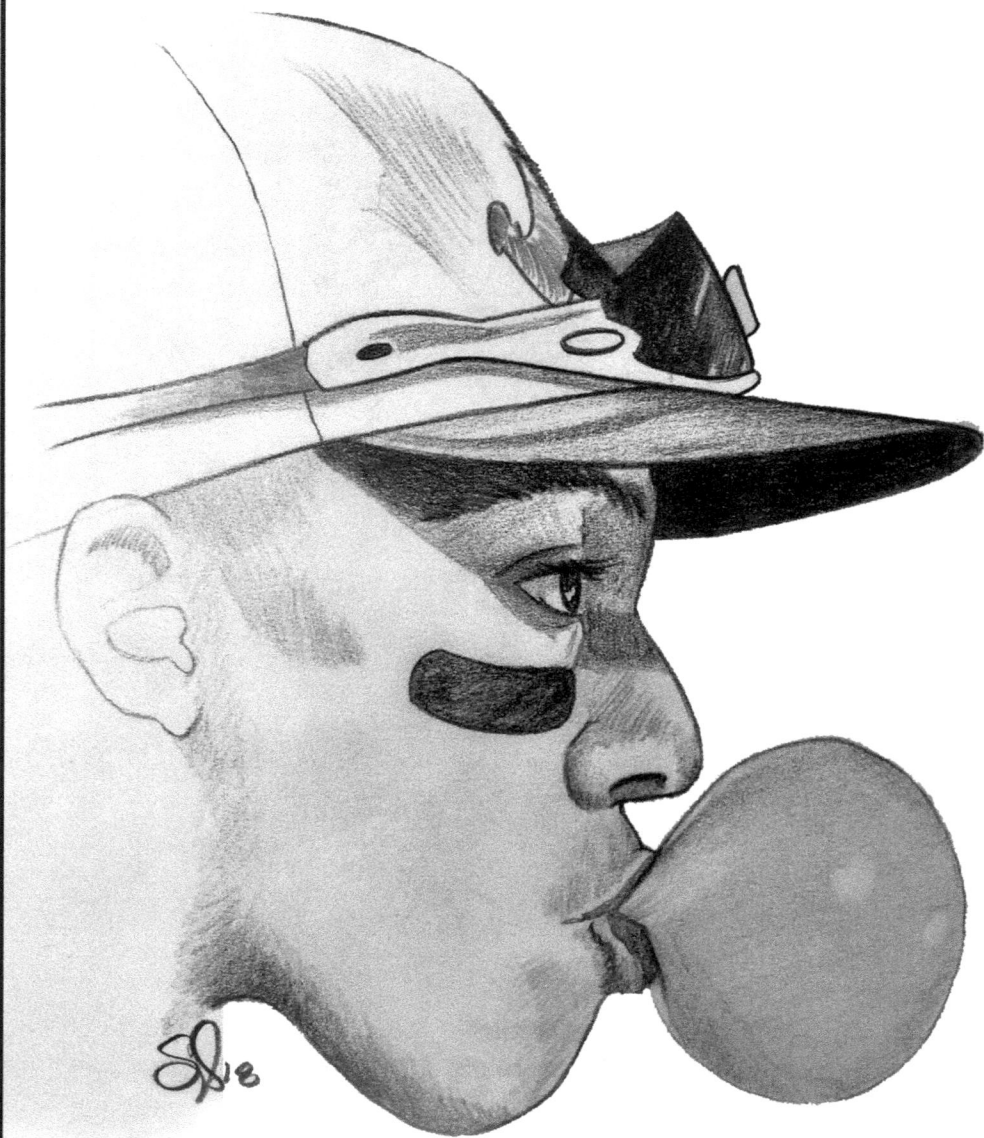

Do you like the 7th inning stretch?
Is that when you get more snacks?
Ya' like salty or sweet, more hotdogs
with nacho cheese?

Oh, be careful or you'll spill it on your lap!

What's your *faaaavorite*
baseball memory?
What's your *faaaavorite* all time game?

W ho's your **dream** team?
Who'd you like to meet?
Who's an *All-Star* in this game?

Is it Jeter, Mickey, Jackie, or Cruz?
Is it Griffey, is it Bonds, is it Maris or Lou?
Could it be Nolan or what about the Babe?

What NAMES the *Legends* have made!

Can YOU name some big parks?
GO AHEAD, Try it right here...

_____ *Field*

_____ *Park*

_____ *Stadium*

_____ *Yard*

You DID IT! That's GREAT to hear!

*N*ow what's YOUR favorite *Ballpark*?
Name it smack dab RIGHT here...

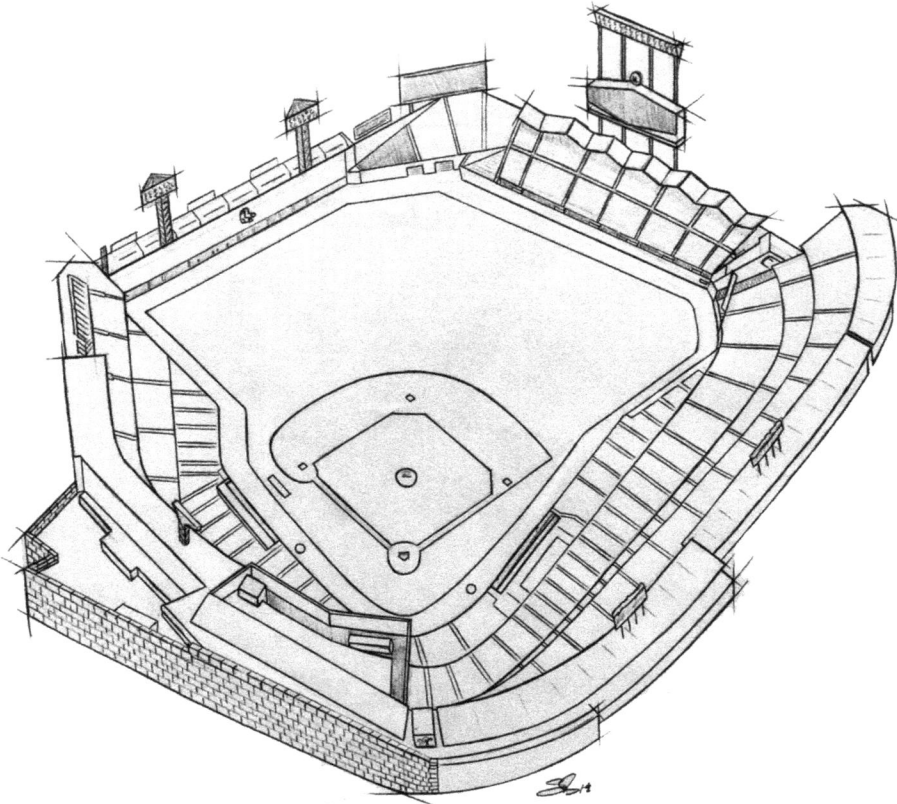

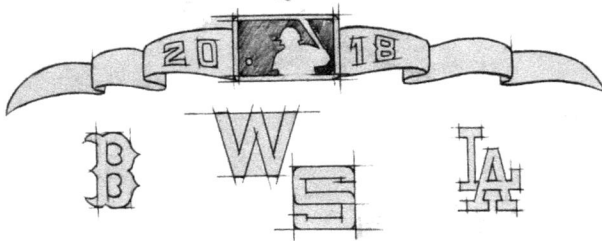

_____

20 18

B W S LA

Even if I'm not ON a team,
I CAN still play.

I can *throw*.
I can *catch*.
I can *swing*.
I can *pitch*.

I can *Play* anywhere, ANY DAY!

I'm a baseball *Fan*.
I think it's super swell.
I love EVERYTHING about
Baseball so thank you
for letting me tell.

I'm a baseball fan, I LOVE to **baseball dream.** So, shout out to the players and shout out to the teams.

*T*hank you for answering my questions and sharing a

Baseball Dream!

Now, *Let's Play Ball!*

What has eighteen legs and catches flies?

www.ingramcontent.com/pod-product-compliance
Lightning Source LLC
Chambersburg PA
CBHW062009090426
42811CB00005B/801